LITTLE LEAGUE

Published by Creative Education, Inc.

123 South Broad Street, Mankato, MN 56001

Designed by Rita Marshall with the help of Thomas Lawton

Cover illustration by Rob Day, Lance Hidy Associates

Photography by Allsport, Bettmann Archive, Duomo,
Anthony Neste, Seitz and Seitz, Wide World Photos,
Terry Wild Studio

Printed in the United States

Library of Congress Cataloging-in-Publication Data

Berry, S. L.

Little League / Skip Berry.

Summary: Presents highlights from the Little League World
Series, an event held annually since 1947 in Williamsport,
Pennsylvania, which features young people's baseball teams
from around the globe.

ISBN 0-88682-538-5

1. Little League World Series, Williamsport, Pa.—History
—Juvenile literature.   [1. Little League World Series,
Williamsport, Pa.—History.   2. Baseball—History.]
1. Title.

GV880.5.B47   1992
796.357'62—dc20

92-4112
CIP
AC

LITTLE LEAGUE

SKIP BERRY

CREATIVE EDUCATION INC.

4

For one week every August, a quiet town in central Pennsylvania becomes an international city. Tens of thousands of visitors from throughout the world crowd into Williamsport, filling up hotels and motels for fifty miles around. As vivid as a fistful of new crayons, banners and flags festoon storefronts and street corners. Signs in French, German, Spanish, and Chinese welcome visitors.

The world comes to Williamsport, Pennsylvania, for the Little League World Series. It's a week's worth of exciting play-offs between teams from around the globe, capped by the thrilling matchup of the final two teams in the internationally televised championship game.

In 1989, almost forty thousand fans jammed Howard J. Lamade Stadium to watch a team from Kaohsiung, Taiwan, take on a squad from Trumbull, Connecticut, for the World Series championship. The game was a contest between Kaohsiung's pitcher Lee Chien-Chih, whose wicked submarine pitch often sent batters back to the bench shaking their heads, and Trumbull's Chris Drury, whose junkball pitches kept batters guessing.

The Howard J. Lamade Stadium.

After watching Chien-Chih's style the first time through the batting lineup, the boys from Connecticut learned to move up in the batter's box and connect with the ball at the top of its arc. They connected often enough to give Trumbull a 2-1 lead by the bottom of the third inning.

In the meantime, Drury's junkball throws kept the Taiwanese players in check, holding their normally powerful hitting to a minimum.

By the fourth inning, Trumbull had begun to rumble. A single by Dan McGrath led to an error by Kaohsiung's third baseman, which resulted in Trumbull loading the bases. With two outs, Drury bopped a blooper to left field, driving in two runs. In the fifth inning, Trumbull's Ken Martin homered to make it 5-1.

Sun Chao-Chi, a player for the Far East in the 1990 series.

Little League games last six innings rather than nine, so there wasn't much time left. Kaohsiung rallied briefly with another run, but Drury managed to maintain control of the game by keeping batters off balance. After giving up a walk in the top of the sixth, Drury retired the next two.

Then it happened. A Kaohsiung batter read a Drury pitch just right, lofting the ball out of the infield.

With forty thousand pairs of eyes focused on him, Trumbull's left fielder McGrath faded back and waited. White as an egg against the blue August sky, the baseball hung in the air above him. McGrath's teammates watched him watch the ball, and they held their breath. If he caught it, the game would be over. And for the first time in six years, a U.S. team would win the Little League World Series.

Fifty years before, the founders of Little League baseball never dreamed it would become such an international sensation.

THE BEGINNING

Carl Stotz was an easygoing employee of a Williamsport sandpaper factory. When his nephews, six-year-old Jimmy and eight-year-old Harold Gehron, complained that older boys in the neighborhood wouldn't let them play baseball, twenty-nine-year-old Stotz promised he'd find a way for them to play on a team.

Bobby Shannon of Shippensburg, Pennsylvania.

He approached Bert and George Bebble, brothers who had once played semipro ball, and asked for their help in organizing a baseball league for youngsters. Together the three men developed three teams, located sponsors to pay for uniforms and equipment, and created a playing schedule.

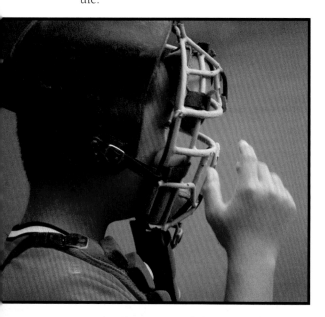

The first game of the new league was played on June 6, 1939, and pitted Lundy Lumber against Lycoming Dairy on a field owned by Stotz's employer. Lundy Lumber's sluggers overwhelmed their opponents 23-8.

Little League baseball caught on quickly in the United States and around the world.

Over the next few years the concept of organized baseball for youngsters caught on, and Little League became popular throughout the area. Each Little League program was organized by districts, and by 1947 there were sixty teams in fifteen leagues in two states—Pennsylvania and New Jersey. That was enough to hold a tournament, Stotz thought.

9

In 1947, the first Little League World Series competition was held. Then called the National Little League Tournament, it was played at Memorial Park in Williamsport. Eleven teams were involved that year, and after elimination rounds were completed the Maynard (Pennsylvania) Midgets faced the Lock Haven (Pennsylvania) Little League in the championship game.

"It was a natural rivalry," recalled former Maynard outfielder Jack Losch years later. "Our towns had matched up against each other in football and basketball for many years."

More than twenty-two hundred people turned out to watch the action, sitting on cars and sprawling in the grass. The players, wearing wool uniforms and ankle-high canvas sneakers, were uncomfortable in the muggy August heat. The game seesawed for a while until the Midgets found their rhythm and soundly beat Lock Haven 16-7.

"The game went back and forth, and we were all filled with butterflies," remembered Losch, who eventually gave up baseball to play professional football for the Green Bay Packers. "Every time Lock Haven got a hit, we were all pulling for our teammates to make the play. Every time one of us was at bat, we were all coaching him to get a hit. It was a total team effort."

Rodney Halter played for the Eastern regional champs in 1990.

A 1910 sandlot game in New York City.

A GREAT TRADITION

As Little League baseball spread throughout the United States and the rest of the world, the National Little League Tournament became the Little League World Series. Today, seven thousand leagues in twenty-nine countries vie to send teams to Williamsport.

Teams in those leagues play approximately 12,250 regular-season games over a seven-week period; each league then chooses an All-Star team of fourteen players to compete in one of 450 district tournaments. Winners of those tournaments meet in section tournaments, which narrow the race to 150 section champs. From those teams come fifty state champions in the United States, plus their equivalents in other countries. Finally, regional tournaments determine the eight teams that will meet in Williamsport for the World Series championship rounds. The final teams represent Little League baseball's eight regions—four in the United States (East, West, Central, and South) and four in other parts of the world (Canada, Latin America, Europe, and the Far East).

Through the years, the young players on those series teams have treated the world to plenty of great moments.

Aron Garcia pitched a no-hitter for his El Cajon, California, team in 1987.

Cominski swung once . . . "Strike one!" yelled the umpire. He swung again . . . "Strike two!"

Everyone knew that sooner or later someone on one of the teams was going to score the winning run—and in sudden death, one run is all it takes to clinch a victory. Cominski watched the mound as the pitcher wound up. His arm snapped forward—another fastball!

Cominski stepped into it, and his bat met the ball with a crack, lifting it high into the sky and out beyond the fence. Home run! As his teammates whooped and hollered, Cominski trotted around the bases, making Morrisville the World Series champs.

MEXICO'S CHAMPIONS

When it comes to glorious moments in Little League history, few match the 1957 championship win by a ragtag team from Monterrey, Mexico. Chosen from teams in the Monterrey Industrial League, the World Series squad was made up of impoverished youngsters who grew up playing baseball barefooted. For many of them, their Little League uniforms and shoes were the first new clothes they'd ever owned.

For instance, there was the 1955 championship game, which is still regarded as one of the most dramatic contests in series history. Pitting a team from Morrisville, Pennsylvania, against one from Delaware Township, New Jersey, the game went into sudden-death overtime with a 3-3 score. Baseball legend Cy Young, who was eighty-eight years old, was among the crowd watching from the sidelines as Morrisville's Richard Cominski came to bat. It was the bottom of the seventh inning, with two outs and no one on base.

Delaware Township's pitcher had a wicked fastball, which had left several Morrisville batters swinging at empty air.

At the time, to earn a berth in the World Series, all foreign teams had to compete in U.S. regional tournaments. As they made their way north, winning games in Texas and Kentucky, the Mexican players also won plenty of support. Their spirited play on the field, and their lively spirits off, inspired people wherever they went to offer meals, lodging, and transportation.

Jesu Contreras, catcher for the Monterrey (Mexico) 1957 world champions, gets pointers from Dodger catcher Roy Campanella.

By the time they made it to Williamsport, the Mexican players had attracted national attention. So when a semifinal game victory sent them to the championship, the boys from Monterrey were the favorites of many Little League baseball fans across the country.

They were also the underdogs, facing a tough team from La Mesa, California, a small town with a big love of Little League baseball. More than thirteen hundred La Mesa youngsters played on the town's sixty-nine Little League teams. La Mesa's World Series team was filled with excellent players.

The World Series brings all nations together.

Size was a problem for the Monterrey team—the largest player was five feet, three inches tall, while most of the others stood less than five feet tall and weighed an average of eighty pounds. Many of La Mesa's players towered over their Mexican rivals, and outweighed them. The La Mesans were also stronger.

However, the Mexican team had Angel Macias, who was not only a switch-hitter, but a switch-pitcher as well. He could throw equally well right- or left-handed, though he never switched pitching arms during a game. He was also a talented infielder and batter. Of his many skills, none was more crucial in the championship game than his pitching.

For the first four innings neither team could get the edge. Then, in the fifth, speedy base running and a couple of La Mesa errors gave Monterrey a 4-0 lead.

Angel Macias, talented switch-pitcher and switch-hitter for the Monterrey team.

Throughout the game, Macias held his own on the mound. Pitching right-handed, he left the Californians blinking as he struck out eleven of eighteen batters. Of those La Mesa players who got a piece of the ball, none made it to base thanks to Monterrey's excellent infield defense. By the time he retired the final La Mesan, Macias had pitched the first perfect championship game in series history, giving up no walks, no hits, and no runs. Monterrey won the 1957 World Series 4-0.

President Dwight Eisenhower, whose grandson was a Little Leaguer, invited the Mexican team to Washington, D.C., where they visited him at the White House. When they finally returned to Mexico, the new champions were greeted at Mexico City's airport by forty thousand cheering fans. Angel Macias was named Mexico's Athlete of the Year, an honor usually reserved for adults.

Good fielding can be the key to victory.

The next year Monterrey again sent a team to Williamsport, but thirteen-year-old Macias was too old to play. Led instead by the pitching of Hector Torres, the Mexican team won the 1958 World Series, making it the first Little League team to win consecutive championships. Though Macias never grew large enough to make a major league team, Torres went on to play shortstop for the Houston Astros.

Angel Macias celebrates Monterrey's 1957 victory on his teammates' shoulders.

A third Monterrey team made it to the 1964 World Series, but lost the championship game to a feisty team from Staten Island, New York. Staten Island pitching ace Danny Yacarino threw a no-hitter and hit a home run to help clinch his team's victory. Ironically, the final score, 4-0, was the same as the score in Monterrey's 1957 victory. Back in New York, the Staten Island champs received heroes' welcomes, including a ticker-tape parade through the streets of Manhattan.

Chen Chien-Wei is one in a long line of superb Far East players.

FAR EASTERN VICTORY

In 1967 a team from West Tokyo, Japan, became the first Far Eastern team to win the World Series. Though skies were cloudy the day of the championship game, the Japanese players dazzled spectators with tremendous fielding and defense as they held their opponents from Chicago, Illinois, to only three hits and one run. Midway through the game, West Tokyo's center fielder Kenichi Tsuchiya, who was the smallest player in the game, whacked a 220-foot home run. The final score of the game was 4-1.

That victory marked the beginning of the Far Eastern region's dominance of the World Series. In 1968 a team from Wakayama, Japan, won the championship. The following year the Taipei Golden Dragons became the first team from Taiwan to win a World Series; over the next twenty-one years, twelve more Taiwanese teams would do the same.

One of the hardest-fought Taiwanese victories came in the 1971 championship game in which a team from Tainan, Taiwan, defeated a team from Gary, Indiana, by a 12-3 score, a misleading margin of victory. Lasting nine innings, the game took two hours and fifty-one minutes to play, making it the longest in tournament history. It was also the first game in which an all-black team (the Gary squad) played for the World Series title.

The Gary team was more than a match for the superbly trained, well-disciplined Taiwanese. During World Series week in Williamsport, ace pitcher and power hitter Lloyd McClendon's five official at-bats resulted in five home runs, each one hit off the first pitch!

Another notable player on the Gary squad was four foot, five inch Kenny Hayes. Known as Squeaky, he bounced around in his third-base coaching box signaling batters. According to Ray Keyes, the sports editor of the *Williamsport Sun-Gazette,* Hayes's antics made him a crowd favorite: "Squeaky would put his hands on his hips to start an inning. Next he'd give the sign. He'd look pretty dejected if a batter didn't follow his signal. He'd use both hands to illustrate how a batter should swing."

A strategic bunt.

The championship game was a pitching duel, a display of ball control and iron nerves by two strong young athletes. Tainan's Hsu Chin-mu pitched magnificently, striking out twenty-two batters. However, McClendon wasn't among that number; after he hit a three-run homer in the first inning, Chin-mu intentionally walked McClendon throughout the rest of the game.

At the same time, McClendon allowed Tainan only three hits and three runs before finally running out of steam. In the top of the ninth, after walking two batters and allowing a single, he removed himself from the game.

That's when the Taiwanese team took over. Sending fourteen batters to the plate, the Far Eastern regional champs turned seven singles, four walks, and a fielding error into nine runs. When Gary finally stepped back up to the plate, the long game had worn the young players down and they couldn't muster the energy to battle back. Tainan won the World Series championship title, but the U.S. Central Region champs had made them earn it.

East meets West: Scott Thrush (left) and Kuo Wen-Chu at the 1990 championship.

As for McClendon, he returned home to Gary and continued honing his baseball skills. In 1987, after seven years in the minors, he was added to the roster of the Cincinnati Reds.

MORE GREAT GAMES

Among longtime fans, the 1979 championship game remains one of the great moments in Little League World Series history. Pitting a team of light-haired lightweights from Campbell, California (known as the Campbell Clones because all the players looked so much alike), against a team of taller, heavier youngsters from Pu-tzu Town, Taiwan, the game was an eight-inning display of superb baseball.

"For sheer enjoyment," broadcaster Red Barber said afterwards, "I can't recall anything to top that game. Those kids . . . enjoyed playing the game. It was a joy to watch the way they played. They would throw to the right base and make the right play at the right time."

The terrific pitching of Dai Hanchao, who struck out seventeen on his way to a no-hitter, finally helped Pu-tzu Town eke out a 2-1 win.

Sliding home.

Due to the excellence of Japanese and Taiwanese teams, by the time the 1982 World Series rolled around no American team had won the championship since 1975. Pu-tzu Town again sent a team to Williamsport, and was favored by many to give Taiwan its sixth championship in a row. That was before Cody Webster and his teammates from Kirkland, Washington, showed up, ready to play ball.

That's exactly what they did. With Webster, a sturdy twelve-year-old, on the mound throwing seventy-five-mile-per-hour fastballs, the Kirkland team treated baseball fans to another thrilling Little League World Series championship game.

It didn't start off as well as it ended, however. Nervousness and the noise of 36,500 spectators chanting "U.S.A.! U.S.A.!" led Webster to walk one batter and go to a full count on several others in the first inning. To settle himself down, Webster said later, he made himself ignore the crowd.

The pitcher controls the pace of the game.

"I really wanted to win bad," he recalled, "and I knew we could do it. I began to concentrate on the catcher's glove instead of everything else that was happening, and from then on I was all right."

Jim Playford, manager of the European team, instructs his players.

A close call at the plate.

Neither team scored until the third inning, when a Kirkland runner on third base made it home on a safety squeeze bunt. In the following inning, Kirkland jumped to a 4-0 lead on a pair of RBI singles and a defensive error, the fourth such error committed by the normally unflappable Taiwanese team.

Heading for first.

In the sixth inning, Webster added to his extraordinary series performance by striking out the side one-two-three. When the home-plate umpire called the third strike on the third Pu-tzu Town batter, Webster threw his glove into the air and the crowd roared. In all, during his week in Williamsport, Webster struck out twenty-six batters in twelve innings and compiled a single, two doubles, a home run, and three RBI.

A home-plate showdown.

Webster stepped to the plate in the fifth inning and blasted Pu-tzu Town hurler Chen Chin-Tung's first pitch over the center-field fence. By the time the ball stopped bouncing, it had gone to the foot of the stadium's scoreboard, 280 feet from the batter's box, making it the longest hit in Little League World Series history. After the game David Bennett, a Williamsport youngster who retrieved the ball, caught up with Webster and gave it to him as a memento of that historic homer.

Kirkland not only beat the Taiwanese team, they shut them out 6-0. While elated Kirkland players danced around the diamond exchanging high fives, their opponents (many with tears in their eyes) shook hands with the new World Series champs. It was a moving display of the type of sportsmanship Little League officials encourage in young ballplayers.

OLD CHAMPS AND NEW

In 1987, the fortieth anniversary of the Little League World Series attracted over thirty-five thousand people, including the members of the first championship team, the Maynard Midgets. A team reunion brought together former Maynard players, many of whom hadn't seen one another for forty years.

The championship game that year was a contest between another powerhouse team from Taiwan, Hua Lian, and the U.S. West Region champs from El Cajon, California. The Taiwanese team was led by crack hitter Pan Yu-long, who smashed two balls over the fence, one for a grand-slam home run. Yu-long's skill with a bat was especially painful for El Cajon's pitcher Aron Garcia, who was regarded as perhaps the best twelve-year-old pitcher in the United States. Garcia's arm was no match for the Taiwanese, who scored at will, running up a final tally of 21-1, the largest winning margin in series history. Hua Lian's win marked the twelfth championship title for Taiwanese teams in fourteen trips to Williamsport.

1987 marked the twelfth time a team from Taiwan won the Little League championship.

The Trumbull players celebrate their 1989 title.

THE LAST OUT

On a hot afternoon in 1989 the left fielder for Trumbull, Connecticut, Dan McGrath, watched the fly ball above him as the batter from Kaohsiung, Taiwan, headed down the baseline. The ball reached the top of its arc and spiraled down. McGrath was ready.

In a championship game, there's no sweeter sound than the smack of a fly ball landing in a leather glove for the final out. McGrath heard that smack and closed his glove.

He leaped into the air, yelping with joy. His teammates leaped on each other, whacking backs and holding their index fingers in the air. Howard J. Lamade Stadium erupted with cheers.

Fourteen boys from Trumbull, Connecticut, had just beaten an outstanding team from Kaohsiung, Taiwan, to win the 1989 Little League World Series. It was another in a long list of great moments.